How to Practice Music

Andrew Eales

ISBN: 978-1-70515-961-3

HAL•LEONARD®

Visit Hal Leonard Online at
www.halleonard.com

Contact us:
Hal Leonard
7777 West Bluemound Road
Milwaukee, WI 53213
Email: info@halleonard.com

In Europe, contact:
Hal Leonard Europe Limited
42 Wigmore Street
Marylebone, London, W1U 2RY
Email: info@halleonardeurope.com

In Australia, contact:
Hal Leonard Australia Pty. Ltd.
4 Lentara Court
Cheltenham, Victoria, 3192 Austrália
Email: info@halleonard.com.au

About the Author

One of the UK's most influential music educationalists, Andrew Eales is based in Milton Keynes, where he runs a successful piano-teaching studio. He is a published composer and author, and his compositions and recordings have been streamed more than a million times.

Andrew has worked as a consultant for several leading educational organizations and examination boards. An acclaimed speaker, he has trained and worked alongside teachers across the UK, North America, and Africa. His video feedback service now provides affordable, expert help and guidance for piano players the world over.

Andrew is renowned for his piano education website pianodao.com, which includes hundreds of free articles and reviews to support piano players and teachers worldwide.

www.pianodao.com

Foreword

Whatever our aspiration as a musician happens to be, the wonderful and endless journey on which we embark in that pursuit will inevitably include the activity we call "practice." It's the word that describes the time we devote to forming a relationship with our chosen instrument or voice. And there's no escaping it if we wish to develop that relationship into something meaningful. Through practice, we can develop the ability to play or sing for our own pleasure, for the pleasure of others, and to take part in whatever appropriate social music-making is available.

Most of us will probably practice a lot more than we perform. And that's a fact for both the seasoned concert artist and the serious amateur. So, it's really important that we enjoy practicing and use whatever time we devote to it as effectively as we can.

That's where *How to Practice* comes in. In this eminently readable and succinct guide, Andrew Eales has addressed all issues relating to practicing. Having carefully considered the material in this book, you will feel both informed and confident whatever your instrument or voice. Your practice will inevitably become more enjoyable and effective.

In its thoughtfully laid-out 50 sections, you will surely find every question you could have about your practice concisely and helpfully answered. And within those answers, you will find much wise advice and many practical suggestions.

We should always strive to find joy and delight in practicing. This book will be a great help in enabling that very worthy intention.

Paul Harris

Preface

Where Does Music Come From?

Perhaps this is a rather odd question. But it is one well worth thinking about before we go further. Pressed for an answer, some will suggest that music comes from the instrument. But that somewhat diminishes the importance of both player and practice. Going further, others will offer that music comes from their movements, fingers, mouth, or breath. Digging still deeper, they might suggest that music comes "from the heart." We could even conclude that music is derived from the mind, psyche, intention, or creative spark.

What Is Practice?

Practice is the process of enhancing any or all of these music-making sources. The result of good practice is that we are able to fully express ourselves musically.

Many excellent books consider an instrument or voice in specific detail, explaining how to hold a bow, improve embouchure, or position fingers. This book will be considering the bigger picture. How can we all practice better?

How to Use This Book

This book will introduce a host of activities, strategies, and approaches that I hope will help you find happiness and engagement in your practice.

However strong our impetus for music-making, the self-discipline and rigor of the practice room can potentially steal our joy and rob us of our potential. So, be kind to yourself. You won't be able to apply everything here all at once and nor should that concern you. Just keep coming back for reminders, inspiration, and fresh help as and when you need it.

You may read this cover to cover, although that is not necessarily the intention. Rather, *How to Practice Music* is a reference source to accompany you on your musical journey over many years. Different parts will become relevant at different points along that journey. Treat what follows as a candy store, from which you can pick and mix the ideas that work for you. Then, use research, exploration, and imagination to go deeper.

It's recommended that you avoid compartmentalizing this book's topics. Experiment in combining a spectrum of suggestions into creative, engaging activities. Holistic learning is deeper learning. By making better connections between activities, you will foster your own art of practice.

Wherever you are in your musical journey, this book will give you a better idea of how to practice music, good reasons for doing so, and the confidence to succeed.

Andrew Eales

Contents

How to Be Motivated

Why Do We Practice?

Ask musicians why we spend long hours practicing and you'll hear a multitude of answers:

- To get better at playing
- To improve a piece that I am learning
- To prepare for an exam or performance
- To complete the work a teacher has set
- To be ready for the next band practice

These are all good reasons. It's interesting that the one answer rarely given is:

> "Because I really enjoy the effort and
> the process of practicing"

Having decided that we want to make music, isn't it odd that we don't always enjoy spending time practicing or even feel like bothering? There are several possible reasons for this.

- We may be struggling with time management or have taken on too many commitments.
- We may feel bored with the music we are practicing or complacent because it isn't suitably challenging.
- We might feel overwhelmed by too high a musical challenge, lacking confidence in our ability and confused about how to progress.
- We might be frustrated that we haven't improved as quickly as we expected and are unsure about how to recalibrate our expectations.

Lurking in the background is the possibility that we simply **don't know how to practice music**. In the Preface, we suggested that "practice" is everything we do to realize our communicative goals as musicians. We practice to communicate better. So, how can we practice better?

Be Inspired

To start with, we should want to practice. But to be motivated, we need goals, aspirations, or deadlines.

When You Don't Feel Like Practicing

Reflect on why you first wanted to learn an instrument, how far you have progressed already, and what you enjoy most about playing.

Gather momentum. The better we practice, the more we progress. As we progress, the more we (and others) will enjoy our playing.

Consider how the truth of this affects you.

- Would you enjoy playing more if you progressed more quickly?
- How much more could you practice than you presently do?
- Do your practice sessions leave you feeling happy, motivated, and inspired?

Let go of disappointment. If you have experienced a setback or feel frustrated, try to stay calm and reflect on how to learn from both your successes and failures. Momentary failure sucks but don't let it define you. For many, the greatest catalyst to success is often failure.

Plan. Practice sessions with goals and a purpose are rewarding. If you have your instrument, music books, and any other equipment ready in advance it will help with getting started. If you need strategies for planning, you'll find them in the chapter "How to Plan Your Practice."

Reward yourself. Charge your motivation with an external boost by promising yourself a special treat if you achieve a particular practice goal.

Hang out with other musicians. Spending time with like-minded music lovers adds a social element that is too often missing in our practice journey.

Motivation (Inside Out)

There are many external factors and circumstances that can motivate our practice, including:

- Performance exams and other assessments
- Taking part in a music festival or competition
- Preparing for an audition
- Getting ready for an orchestra, band, or choir rehearsal
- Receiving teacher rewards, such as candy or stickers
- Tick lists and challenges
- The need for praise from others
- An impending concert
- Receiving payment

These can all be positive goals to work for. However, some studies suggest that if we are only motivated by external factors, our internal love of music may be weakened.

Consider which of these statements you identify with. Then, try saying them aloud. Use this process to affirm your personal reasons for practicing.

- I enjoy listening to music; it is important in my life.
- If I am unable to play my instrument for a few days, I miss it.
- I like to choose the music I play.
- When I play well, I feel a sense of satisfaction.
- I like to play music for myself, whether anybody else listens or not.
- I am curious to discover new music and new styles of music.
- I like to challenge myself as a player.
- Playing music helps me to feel positive about myself.
- I like to play pieces my way and it doesn't matter whether others agree with my interpretations.
- I enjoy creating my own music, improvising, and composing.

More Tips for Motivation

Make a "to-do" list of all the other things crowding for your attention. Plan to go back to all those thoughts and tasks later. Now, put the list down and go practice!

Other than digital music, practice resources, and time-telling aids, put your electronic devices aside for the duration of your practice. They will distract you. (Can you hold a meaningful conversation with a friend while staring at your phone every two minutes?) Your time to practice should be sacrosanct. If you need devices in the room, switch off the notifications.

Recruit a "practice buddy," preferably a friend who plays at a similar level and can commit to an equal amount of time. You can aim to coordinate your session times, hold each other to account, or simply check in once a week.

If practicing is an ongoing chore, it's probably time to try shaking up your routine. Here are some suggestions of ways to do this.

- Mix up when and/or where you practice.
- Change the music you are learning.
- If you have a set practice schedule, vary the order and length of your day-to-day activities.
- Spend plenty of time playing "for fun" without specific goals or targets.
- Listen (lots) to your favorite music and musicians, nourishing yourself with musical inspiration.

Try stopping when you've barely started your planned practice session. This triggers a phenomenon known as "resumptive drive" (or the "Zeigarnik effect"). You'll be itching to get back to your practice as soon as possible!

And remember, a little bit of practice is better than nothing at all. We don't experience our victories daily. Rather, they gather steam over time.

How to Plan Your Practice

How Much Should I Practice?

This is one of the most commonly asked questions from students, parents, and adult learners.

A mischievous answer would be to suggest "as little as possible."

It is important to understand that we need to focus on our goals and outcomes, rather than clock-watching. It's a cliché that practice is about quality not quantity. But it's the truth.

Alongside this basic response, there are two other key points to bear in mind.

1. Firstly, there is much evidence to suggest that short, focused, and daily practice sessions achieve much more than occasional binge practicing.
2. Secondly, we should recognize that treating practice as an extended play activity rather than as scheduled work might have a transformational impact on our development and progress.

Contradictions? Combine the two approaches below for fulfilled and productive practice.

1. Daily, focused practice sessions, each with carefully planned goals.
2. When time allows, longer sessions of an hour or more where you can become completely absorbed in your curiosity and love of music.

Now, let's look at these two approaches in greater detail.

The Two Types of Practice Session

As you read through this book, it will become clear that practicing music involves a significant range of activities that together would take up more time than most of us could commit.

To help you focus on a manageable but effective practice strategy, it can help to think of two types of session.

1. The Routine Session

This is ideally a daily fixture and might range in length from about ten minutes to an hour depending on your level and lifestyle.

Try to fix a regular time for the routine session, for example first thing in the morning, during a lunch break, after school or work, or simply at a time that works around the activities of those you live with.

The routine session benefits from having a specific focus or goal and could include different activities each day. Make sure that across the whole week you cover all the elements of practice that are important to your ongoing progress.

Try to integrate related activities (e.g., spending a session sight reading and improvising in the same key).

2. The "Deep Dive"

Try a longer, more absorbing, and playful practice session, preferably once a week. This "deep dive" into your musical journey can be a more varied and absorbing session of an hour or more and might include a variety of musical activities or focus on a single piece that is proving challenging.

In a "deep dive," you might find yourself revisiting your favorite pieces from the past, working on a skill or technique, or improvising and composing your own music. Avoid planning these sessions in advance. Instead, find out where your playful curiosity takes you.

Making Time for Your Practice

Life can be busy. But to enjoy satisfying music-making, regular practice is important. Here are some useful tips for making time for practicing music.

Schedule practice sessions and try to stick to a regular time each day. This is the first, key step to quicker progress and greater enjoyment.

Schedule other activities, too! This is the big one. If you list and timetable your other activities, you may well be surprised at how much "free" time appears in your schedule.

Be smart with the time you have. When you can only grab ten minutes to practice, know what you would like to achieve in that time. Write a list of what you will do and for how long. Halfway through a "bitesize" practice session, quickly check whether you have made a good start towards your goal. Do this again at the end.

Ask for support. Honest communication is vital. Let family, partners, and friends know that you need private time to practice your instrument and that it is important to you. See what you can do to support them with their interests and chosen activities in return.

Make the most of multitasking. In its broadest sense, "practice" can involve spending time listening to and researching music. This be done on the way to school or work, between tasks, or even during other activities.

Keep your instrument available and ready. If you play a smaller instrument such as the violin, flute, or ukulele, take it with you when you can. With larger instruments, keep them set up and always ready to play. For example, if you are a piano student, why not knock out a few scales each time you pass the open piano in your home? These micro-practice moments quickly add up and the progress you make may surprise you.

When you reflect on this chapter and try to summarize your life interests in a timetable, you may conclude that your expectations are unrealistic. If you need to re-evaluate your priorities, do so with care and in conversation with those closest to you.

Where to Practice

Where do you go to practice?

Depending on the instrument you play and your living accommodation, the answer to that question may vary considerably. But regardless of precisely where you practice, here are some guidelines for making the most of the space you have.

Firstly, during the course of your practice, the space should be **private** and **undisturbed**. The anticipation of being disturbed or observed by others, however supportive, can make us become self-conscious. This experience is known as "evaluation apprehension." Practicing is not as productive in this context.

The room needs to be **quiet**. This is to both avoid distraction and enable you to properly hear the detail of your playing. Consider also the impact that a room's acoustics will have on tone, articulation, and dynamics.

There needs to be **enough space** to move as required.

The **temperature** and **humidity** in the room need to be comfortable for the player and optimal for the instrument. Seek advice about the latter from a manufacturer or technician.

Suitable **lighting** is helpful to avoid eyestrain. Consider using a spotlight.

Air quality is also important, and not only for those who sing or play woodwind and brass instruments. Air quality is understood to impact on our learning and progress, as well as being important for our overall health. Where ventilation is poor, a portable air filter and ioniser can make a significant difference.

Instruments and Equipment

It is difficult to maintain enthusiasm for playing an instrument if you suspect that, despite your best efforts, it is incapable of producing a pleasing sound.

Buy or hire the very best instrument you can afford and keep it in good order. Acoustic pianos should be regularly tuned (a minimum of once every sixth months). Other instruments require maintenance and servicing from a specialist.

Don't wait for somebody else to point out that your instrument is unsuitable or falling apart; be proactive in keeping it in top condition. This is essential for fruitful and rewarding practice.

If you sit on a chair to practice, it is important that the chair used for this purpose will support a healthy posture, permit sufficient freedom of movement, and can be adjusted as needed.

Make sure you keep the following to hand (as required) when practicing:

- Instrument accessories (e.g., spare reeds, strings, or plectrums)
- Notebook and pencil
- Stable, sturdy music stand
- Practice apps and digital accessories
- Metronome
- Instrument tuning device
- Recording device
- Ear plugs, where noise and hearing are an issue
- Drinking water (in a safe place away from your instrument)

A mirror can be useful for checking posture, facial expressions, breathing, and practicing pre-concert talks.

Consideration for Neighbors

Before playing your first note, it's important to consider the time of day and, crucially, your neighbors.

It is a mistake to simply play quietly. When practicing, we need to encounter our instrument's full dynamic range, learning to control it with musicality and imagination.

Here are some suggestions for avoiding conflict.

- **Be considerate**. Do your neighbors work from home, work shifts that require them to sleep at unusual times, or have young children?
- Where possible, try to **work around your neighbors**, ensuring that your music practice takes place at a time less likely to cause serious problems.
- **Communicate**. Ask your neighbors if your music practice disturbs them. Negotiate reasonable compromise but explain that a certain amount of practice is needed most days. Ask when they would prefer longer practice sessions to happen.
- You may consider, where possible, switching to playing the **digital equivalent** of your instrument and using **headphones**.
- If you play an instrument that is portable, consider practicing at an **alternative venue**.
- If appropriate, you may consider researching into the feasibility and cost of **soundproofing**.

Plan Your Practice

This book outlines a wide range of practice activities. But unless you can enjoy an extended time for practicing, it is unlikely you will include all or even many of them daily.

Your daily, "routine" practice sessions should be preceded by an element of premeditated planning. Avoid going into these without any idea of what you will play or hope to achieve. When planning how you will spend your practice session, remember to include a balanced range of:

- **Core goals**: specific targets set by a teacher, band leader, or required for an upcoming event or exam
- **General development**: broader areas such as technique, music reading, musicianship skills, and a diverse knowledge of repertoire

When starting a longer practice session, times for **warming up** and **breaks** should be included. These are addressed in detail in the sections "How to Warm Up" and "How to Practice Mindfully."

For a more disciplined approach, make a list of what you hope to achieve and how long you plan to spend on each section of practice. At the end of a practice session, you should be able to answer the question "how have I progressed?" easily.

Consider how you can integrate the different elements of your practice; for example, this could be combining scale work, sight reading, improvising, and playing pieces in the same key.

If you are working with a teacher, start by reflecting on what happened in your last lesson and consider how you would like to spend your next lesson.

But remember, practicing music is not all about work. An absorbing, inquisitive approach, and play, are the hallmarks of the most effective practice. Plan for sections of your practice session (or entire sessions) where you enjoy exploring your instrument without premeditated targets.

Practice Notebooks and Journals

Notebooks and journals can be very useful for charting progress, planning practice steps, and recording communication (between teacher, student, and even parent or guardian).

Notebooks for your teacher to write in should be selected by the teacher. Some will be happy to use a simple writing pad, while others will prefer one of the many commercially available notebooks that include spaces for routine information such as a log of practice.

Always consult the notebook at the start of each practice session.

Older learners often like to keep their own journal in which they write a more reflective account of their practice journey, which may or may not ever be shared with a teacher. These can be excellent tools for structuring practice sessions, probing for solutions, or looking back on previous work.

You might buy one of the journals created for different markets such as self-improvement and care. It's possible to adapt one of these or create your own free-prose journal, using the best gift-stationery book you can find.

Taking the idea of a personal journal further, why not keep a digital dossier? As well as charting your progress and storing teacher notes, you can incorporate lists of the music you have listened to, played, performed, and shared. You can also store your compositions, recordings, concert programmes, photos, and more. Such a tool, used well, can become a convenient and flexible compendium of your plans, reflections, and inspirations.

Using Practice Apps

Given the convenience and power of tablet and smartphone apps, you may prefer to plan your practice using a digital app rather than a handwritten notebook.

A good app can offer many features and benefits all in one place.

- Lesson notes, progress charts, and personal journaling space.
- Lists of practice activities, with the option of timing each element.
- Motivational goals, targets, "streaks," badges, and charts.
- Daily check-ins, reminders, and time records of practice sessions.
- Logs for recording your mood, focus, and progress during each session.
- Audio recording and playback.
- Backing tracks for play-along use.
- Built-in digital tuner and/or metronome.
- Synchronization across devices (and even with your teacher).

Using practice apps can be very motivational but requires self-discipline. You will need the app whenever and wherever you practice in order to realize the full benefits; it must become your constant practice companion.

Remember to bear in mind the cost of in-app purchases, data collection, and digital privacy. And don't forget to turn off other notifications on your device while practicing.

As ever, it is a good idea to discuss your use of a practice app with a teacher, your practice buddy, musical friends, or any other support networks you have.

There is likely to be continued growth in the popularity, use, flexibility, and quality offered by digital practice apps. Stay up to date with what is currently available in your device's app store.

Supporting Young Learners

If you are reading this book as a parent or guardian supporting a younger musician, an exciting future awaits, with music sure to become an ever-growing part of your family life.

Of course, it isn't always quite that easy! Even with our best efforts and intentions, supporting children's musical development brings many challenges. **Of these, the importance of instigating a practice routine in the heart of the family home is perhaps the most significant.**

Here are a few points to bear in mind.

- Always be **positive** and **encouraging**. A love of music does not necessarily come together with good time management and self-discipline.
- **Play lots of music recordings** in the home and try to take your child to live concerts if possible. Fan the flame of enthusiasm!
- **Show an interest** in what has been achieved in each practice session, but without judgement. There will be bad days and that's OK.
- With younger children, **sit in and supervise** practice if your child is happy for you to do so. Give them the freedom to experiment. "Play" contributes hugely to effective learning.
- **Talk to your child's teacher** whenever possible; show respect and value their time and advice.
- **Accept** that on some days practice will be tough.
- When there is a lack of practice, explore "why" in a **calm and positive** way. Even the greatest musicians have periods when practice is difficult.
- For very young children, and if the teacher is happy, **be present** in lessons, taking note of the learning and what is set for practice.
- **Supporting** children to practice consistently requires self-discipline and good time management on behalf of the adult, too! Planning, enthusiasm, and effective communication is required of the whole household.

How to Warm Up

Tuning Up, Tuning In

Before we play a single note, we begin with a commitment to practice, closing the door and making a conscious decision to concentrate on the joy of making music.

Bringing our focus to the practice session can be easier if we make our own "ritual" of setting up our instrument, whether that's lifting the piano lid, reaching to take our guitar from its stand, unpacking our instrument from its case, or settling into routine vocal exercises.

Allow all of these to whet your appetite for the music-making to come!

It is helpful to find a musical focal point within any stretches and breathing exercises. Physical preparation is important for all players and can be done either away from or using our instrument. For example:

- Tuning a wind or brass instrument can be combined with bringing our attention to the embouchure
- Stretching can be incorporated with practicing bow hold
- Long notes can be combined with focused breathing exercises

Tuning an instrument will often be an integral element in this "pre-practice ritual." Our approach here can have a big impact on what follows.

Listen to any orchestra or band tune up and you can pick out each player on their own unique tangent, free from the oversight of a score, conductor, or rulebook. Some will seamlessly move into rehearsing technical exercises, revising difficult passages from an upcoming piece, or simply improvising their own playful doodles. The point here is that tuning your instrument is part of "tuning in" for what is to follow, focusing the ear and the mind in preparation for a period of fulfilling music-making. It should be approached with this perspective.

Warming Up

You may have heard the advice that before practicing we should first "warm up."

What Is Warming Up?

Warming up is about physical and mental preparation. Below are listed some elements of warming up that you might want to consider. They will be expanded upon in the next few sections of this book.

Physical Preparation

- Awakening muscles used when playing or singing.
- Stimulating blood circulation (e.g., drawing warmth to the fingers).
- Lubricating joints and releasing tension.
- Deep breathing.

Mental Preparation

- Switching off all distractions.
- Reflecting upon the previous practice session.
- Mapping out or revising practice goals.
- Adjusting expectations.
- Gathering thoughts around the music to be played.

Try not to get stuck in the "warm-up" phase, though! Don't spend more than the first quarter of a practice session warming up.

Physical Stretches

Stretches help **lengthen** muscles, counteracting those daily activities and habits that contract and tense them. Hence, they prepare us for the physical aspect of practicing an instrument.

Spending a couple of minutes on physical stretches at the start and end of a practice session may:

- Encourage effective blood circulation
- Stimulate nerve endings and awaken the senses
- Enable mental focus and clarity

Make sure that your body is warmed up and you are dressed in suitable clothing, avoiding restricting outfits.

For instrument-specific stretches, it is best to check with a specialist or physical therapist. They may be able to recommend bespoke exercises that can be done with your instrument.

Generic stretches that promote a renewed connection between mind, body, and breath are helpful to all musicians, and can be accessed through several modalities and traditions such as yoga, t'ai chi, and qigong.

Be **moderate**. A golden rule when stretching is to stop if it hurts. You should only stretch to around 70–80% of your physical ability.

Stretching should not be forced. It is at its most effective when **practiced gently**.

Breathing

It is accepted wisdom that good breathing habits are vital for all musicians. The pianist András Schiff referred to this as "natural" breathing. **Natural** breathing means **deep** breathing through the diaphragm and into the abdomen. This is opposed to **shallow** breathing, where the breath reaches only into the lungs or chest cavity.

There are many reasons why our breathing habits might not be ideal. In addition to obvious health issues, the quality of our breathing can be influenced by our emotional state, social constraints, and simple practicalities such as tight clothing. All of these can impact on the quality of our practice.

The following will help you to rediscover natural breathing:

- Adopt an alert but relaxed and comfortable posture
- Breathe in and out through your nose
- Notice whether your chest area (lungs) and stomach (abdomen) are both expanding and contracting with each breath
- Simply become conscious of your breathing
- Observe and feel your breathing rather than trying to control it
- Notice the cycle of your breath and adjust its tempo as desired

Healthy breathing has the added benefits of releasing toxins, enlivening cells, and internally massaging the heart and lungs. It can enable greater **focus**, **perspective**, and **productivity** within practice sessions.

A Simple Breathing Exercise

When embarking on a longer practice session, it can be helpful to include a few minutes of structured breathwork.

Rhythmic deep breathing can improve focus, enhance performance, sharpen concentration, and reduce stress, making it the perfect way to prepare for a practice session. It is also an ideal way to spend your break period.

One of the most popular breathwork exercises is sometimes called "box breath" or "four-square breathing." It is as incredibly simple as it is effective. Stand at ease or sit alert in a comfortable chair with your palms in your lap. Close your eyes or else soften your gaze.

- Inhale slowly through the nose, noticing your chest and abdomen expand as you do so (four seconds).
- Pause at the top of your inhale. Try not to tense up (four seconds).
- Gently exhale, releasing your breath without force (four seconds).
- Pause again, resting before the next inhale (four seconds).

You will need either a timer or an app.

Several excellent breathwork apps are available, some of which are free. They usually include a timer, sounds, and visualizations. Some will introduce you to other helpful breathwork exercises if you are interested.

This breathing technique should be attempted for a couple of minutes at first and no longer than five.

Make a conscious note of how you feel after the exercise.

Active Repertoire

It can be very discouraging to feel that we are struggling, making little progress, and lacking what it takes to become a better musician. These feelings can affect anyone, from the beginner to the most experienced artist.

One of the best ways to warm up at the start of practice sessions is to play two or three pieces of **active repertoire**. This helps us to move beyond negative self-talk and positively adjust the balance between **work** and **play**.

Active repertoire is the music we can play any time, any place. These are the pieces we can perform without notice, without any embarrassment, and often from memory.

Too often, players neglect or don't have any active repertoire. But by making it our top priority, we can:

- Start our practice sessions positively, with music that we enjoy playing
- More quickly memorize our favorite pieces
- Overcome our anxiety and feel more at ease playing to others

Here are some tips to help you develop your active repertoire and incorporate it into your practice.

- Play one or more pieces of active repertoire a day if possible. This works best either at the beginning or end of your practice session.
- Try to play without the sheet music. Make a mental note of mistakes and use any uncertainties as a guide for fresh practice.
- Use quiet moments (e.g., before going to sleep, while travelling, or in the bathroom) to play back the "recordings in your head" of active repertoire. This reinforces your memory and enables you to experience them as an audience.

- Go back and study the notated music, looking for details previously missed or neglected.
- Try radically alternative interpretations of active repertoire.
- When playing your active repertoire, visualize an audience and give them your best performance!

Aim to have three pieces you enjoy playing as your active repertoire. Keep a list and regularly revisit it.

This active-repertoire list will evolve as you learn new pieces and discard older ones. But it's great to always have some music that you can play at the drop of a hat. The confidence and self-belief that is gained from enjoying playing this music will help you practice with renewed energy and focus.

How to Practice Core Skills

Scales

Most people agree that many benefits can be gained from practicing and learning scales.

- Scales improve all aspects of physical technique, including fluency, dexterity, intonation, balance, and tone control.
- Scales instil common note patterns for each and every major, minor, modal, blues, and jazz key.
- Scales help us develop a sense of key, harmony, a practical understanding of music theory, and the facility to transpose.
- Scale and chord patterns appear throughout music in all genres, so familiarity with them can considerably speed up the learning of repertoire.
- Scales likewise improve our ability to play new music at sight, making music aurally, physically, and visually more predictable.
- Scales enhance our structural understanding of music (e.g., our awareness of modulation from one key to another).
- Scales are often the foundation for improvisation and composing.

With deeper, cumulative learning, scales can become an embedded language that facilitates the fluency of all our playing. Furthermore, they provide a laboratory in which other techniques and aspects of musicianship can be developed.

For the vast majority of instruments, scales should form part of every scheduled, daily practice session.

Creative Scale Practice

To gain the benefits of scales, we must learn them deeply rather than merely blitzing them for an exam or audition. This involves a process of internalization gained through regular, creative, and musical practice. This will help you develop an **aural** understanding of scales, as opposed to merely playing them by rote.

Here are some ideas that may help you do this.

- On occasion, explore scales **without notation**.
- Scales can be used for creative **experimentation**. Explore different ways of playing them, for example varying the dynamics, articulation, tempo, and mood.
- Try playing scales in **swing** and other rhythmic patterns.
- Use scales as the basis for **improvising** and **composing** music.
- Use scales to address **technical** issues met in the pieces you are practicing (e.g., a particular bow technique or type of articulation).
- Notice where scale **patterns** appear in repertoire and how they are altered to fit the needs of pieces.
- Consider your **breathing** while playing scales, whether or not you play a wind or brass instrument.
- Try to identify any **physical** or **mental tension** when playing through scales.
- Notice when and how pieces change **key** and the role that scales and arpeggios play in melodic patterns and harmony.
- Develop an understanding of the **circle of fifths**; this not only reinforces **theory** knowledge but also enhances **creativity** when improvising and composing.
- Experiment with practicing scales in **short bursts** integrated throughout your practice session, rather than always in a single, self-contained block.

These are just a few simple ideas, a template from which the creative player can use to develop and add many variations. Above all, practice scales **regularly** and **creatively**.

Arpeggios

Arpeggios are just as important as scales, perhaps even more so. They should be practiced with equal **regularity**, using the same **varied** and **creative approach**.

Comprising the intervals of a minor third, major third, and perfect fourth, arpeggios provide a gymnasium of opportunity for developing precision-playing outside of the intervals incorporated by scales.

Playing arpeggios in all the standard keys trains the brain to accurately judge these intervals and provides the opportunity to **develop technical precision**.

Practice arpeggios *legato* and slowly at first, learning to perfect aspects such as intonation, finger patterns, or shifting. Then, develop up to a rapid speed to enhance fluency, dexterity, and musicality.

Broken chords are also important and appear frequently in the music we play. Learn to spot their patterns as they appear in your pieces.

Don't limit yourself or your musical progress by sticking to the requirements of a music **exam syllabus**. These rarely include a sufficient spectrum of arpeggios or broken-chord patterns. Use a thorough scales primer, ask a teacher, post on a trustworthy forum, or develop your own broken-chord patterns to support your technical and musical development.

It can be especially helpful to practice the scale, arpeggio, and broken chord for the home key, dominant, and relative major/minor tonalities of **pieces** you are learning.

Try to practice at least some scales and arpeggios **daily**, towards the start of your practice session after your physical warm up. It can be useful to assign different patterns or keys to each day of the week. You could also play the game "scales from a hat." Write the names of individual scales, arpeggios, and broken chords onto fragments of paper and pop them into a hat (or bowl). Then, pull out individual fragments of paper one by one at random to play. This can be a fun challenge game with your practice buddy, too!

Studies and Exercises

Whether playing piano études by Czerny or the electric guitar exercises of Joe Satriani, musicians have often included additional technical work in their regular practice. Why?

Studies and études are usually based on short musical passages, extended with repetition to systematically explore a specific technique. In many cases, they provide a bridge between pure technical work and the repertoire we play.

To make best use of technical exercises, consider the following.

- If you are unsure of the value of a particular study, don't use it. Studies should be practiced with mindful understanding and in combination with a specific outcome.
- Practice each exercise as directed by a teacher who can explain the specific benefit of a study and offer guidance on its correct use.
- Avoid being obsessive! Exercises can be more physically demanding than you realize, so only use them in moderation and in combination with a specific outcome.
- The more creative we are in the use and adaptation of exercises and studies, the more musically productive and beneficial they are likely to be.
- Practice exercises only when well-rested and on your top form. Used unwisely, they have been known to lead to injury.

In addition to using commercially available material, you can develop and compose your own exercises based on troublesome passages from the pieces you are practicing.

Try to practice exercises from memory, focusing on the physical aspects of playing and the quality of the sound produced.

Music Reading

Just as technique requires structured practice, so does music reading.

One of the main reasons that players often struggle to read fluently is that they spend too little time actually doing it. If you only learn a few pieces and rely on your ear, rote copying, or muscle memory, chances are that you won't be familiarizing yourself sufficiently with the notation on the music stand.

There are several ways to improve our music-reading ability.

- **Learning music theory** in a structured way. This gives us a much better understanding of the notation we are looking at, so we can read it with greater ease.
- **Following sheet music** while listening to recordings and live music. This helps us to properly connect musical sound with the written notation and symbols on the page.
- **Writing music by hand**. Just as handwriting has been shown to facilitate reading acquisition in young children, learning to write music notation by hand can also strengthen music-reading comprehension and note recognition.
- **Making music with others**. Those who regularly play or sing with other musicians using notation invariably develop excellent reading skills.
- **Learning lots of easy "quick-study" pieces.** Learners who attempt a new, easy piece each week without first hearing it quickly improve their reading fluency. Use pieces that are one or two levels easier than your typical repertoire.

Sight Reading

The ability to read and play music notation you haven't seen before is one of the skills that most musicians consider a priority. The sooner you develop this skill, the less likely you are to be frustrated or disappointed later in your development as a musician.

Effortless sight reading develops as we remember musical language and patterns previously encountered. This helps us to anticipate what might come next in a new piece. Good sight-reading materials are specifically designed to foster this process, using all the elements of music notation appropriate to our level.

Here are some tips to help you make productive progress.

Get the Knowledge

Your sight reading will improve immensely if you familiarize yourself with the basics of music theory. Try to memorize and understand:

- Key signatures, including relative major/minor keys
- Scales and arpeggios, which are the patterns at the heart of music
- Time signatures and common rhythmic patterns

Start with Flash Cards

Before trying to sight read passages of music, start with flash cards. Numerous apps are available that replicate flash cards or they can be purchased in music stores or online. You can even make your own.

Use them to develop:

- Recognition of rhythm and short rhythmic patterns using rhythm cards
- Recognition of pitch and short patterns of notes, so that you can instantly name and play or sing any note that might be written for your instrument

Sight read regularly, scheduling specific time within your practice sessions. Avoid "cramming" sight reading for an examination, assessment, or audition. Good sight-reading ability comes simply with regular and varied practice.

Find Suitable Material

Excellent sight-reading resources can be purchased from any music retailer. The major publishers and examination boards offer a range of suitable resources for most instruments. Try to vary the sight-reading resources that you use and the styles of music you sight read.

Have a Good Look First

Spend as long as you need to look through the piece you are about to sight read. It doesn't matter that in an exam context the time might be limited. Apart from in the immediate lead-up to an exam, take plenty of time to assimilate as much information as possible.

Start with the Basics

Be sure to check the key signature. You can usually double-confirm this by looking at the final measure, as most music ends on the keynote, or "tonic." Check the time signature and establish the pulse in your head before looking at the rest of the piece or attempting to play it.

Identify Patterns

When looking through a piece you are about to play at sight, see if you can identify recurring patterns or sequences of notes that follow a similar shape. What are the similarities and differences?

Identify Tricky Sections

Check out where potential problems are likely to occur, such as difficult rhythms, ornaments, finger patterns, or clef changes.

Can You Hear It?

When we read a book silently, we "hear" it mentally. Try to do the same with the music you are about to play. It may help to have a go at humming the music. Pay attention to the expression markings, not just the notes and timing.

Relax and Keep Going!

Just before you begin to play the piece, count yourself in. This will mentally establish the pulse. Then, relax and just keep going. If you make a mistake, choose to ignore it and continue to the next note. Remember that keeping the pulse alive is more important than getting all the notes and other details perfect.

Try a Different Tempo

Players who have a second attempt at a short sight-reading piece very often repeat the same mistakes. Break the cycle by changing the tempo, playing it faster or slower.

Plan It and Stick with It

It is useful to try a sight-reading exercise each day, perhaps midway through your practice for variety. A more extended sight-reading practice can work wonders in terms of building up confidence and fluency. It can also be a good focus for a "deep dive" practice session from time to time.

How Much Can You Remember?

Once you have sight read a passage or piece, try closing the book and seeing how much of it you can remember.

Listen and Evaluate

After having a go at sight reading a piece, listen to a recording or demonstration from a more advanced player. Look at the notation and notice the differences between your own attempt and a more accurate performance. Consider the musical impact and mood of the more polished rendition. Then, have another go at playing the piece yourself.

How to Practice Pieces

Selecting Music to Play

Choosing the right music to play is not easy. But it is perhaps the most important thing to get right if we are to be inspired in our practice and enjoy making music.

We all want to learn new music and often this becomes the focus of our practice. Try to include plenty of variety.

- **Challenge pieces** that we aspire to play but are difficult and stretch our technique, musicianship, and understanding.
- **"Quick-win" pieces** that we can learn in a week or so, building confidence and consolidating our progress.
- **Performance pieces** that we are preparing for a concert or exam.
- **Ensemble pieces** that we will play with other musicians.
- **Quick-study pieces**, whose function is to help us develop our sight-reading ability.
- **"By-ear" pieces** that we try to work out for ourselves without sheet music.
- **Experimental pieces** that introduce us to different styles, genres, and cultures we haven't explored before.
- **Favorite pieces** that we have long enjoyed listening to and have wanted to play.
- **Improvised pieces** that we might develop into new compositions of our own.

Each type of piece listed here suggests a different practice approach. But much of the advice that follows applies equally to all.

Doing Your Research

Before choosing or starting repertoire to practice, it is a good idea to spend plenty of time **listening** to a variety of music and **researching** its origins, context, and background. This will help you play with musical engagement and understanding.

Consider the Level

One of the most important considerations when selecting repertoire is to establish whether the difficulty of the piece is appropriate. Allow for pieces that are easy enough to be enjoyable "quick wins," as well as those that are more challenging and will inspire you to new technical or musical heights.

You can often find out the level of a piece by:

- Checking the **publisher** notes
- Reading independent **reviews** in the music press and online
- Investigating whether it has been selected for a **grade exam**, **federation list**, **audition list**, or equivalent

Avoid committing to learning pieces that are either too easy to engage with or too difficult to ultimately play well.

Does the Music Appeal?

Select music which piques your curiosity and has been recommended by others (such as a teacher, friend, or online).

We rarely progress or enjoy playing music that we wouldn't choose to listen to. However, this doesn't mean that we should stick to a narrow range of "comfort-zone music." It is important and enriching to expand our experience and musical taste. This can only happen when we engage with new music.

Practicing Pieces

Many of the suggestions previously given for sight-reading practice equally apply when learning any piece of music using notation. But now there is no time constraint, nor an embargo on listening to recordings.

Here's a checklist of questions to ask when practicing pieces.

1. **Do I know the background of the piece?** Use the internet and books to find out the context of a piece. Read blog posts, articles, and reference sources for information about the composer and thoughts on how to play the music. Singers should also consider the meaning and translation of lyrics and, if relevant, the wider narrative context of a song (e.g., its place within a musical or opera).

2. **Do I have access to a decent recording of it?** Streaming services all offer a huge wealth of recorded music. In addition to the piece you are learning, check out a composer's other music to get more of a sense of their musical style and personal character.

3. **Do I have a good edition of the sheet music?** An edition that is accurate is essential; don't hesitate to ask for recommendations and read reviews. Unless you are confident in working out your own fingerings, breathing, or bowing, use an edition which includes advice that will make practice easier and more effective.

4. **How does this piece connect to my overall musical learning?** The piece should relate to recent and current musical learning. This might include specific techniques, scales, or rhythms and time signatures that you are working on.

5. **Do I have any questions about the piece or need to clarify anything in the notation?** However independent we may feel we are, we all need a learning support network, whether that is a teacher, mentor, practice buddy, or online community. Don't be afraid to ask for help. You will get further and faster with the support of others.

6. **What are the significant technical challenges?** Know what you are getting into! In addition to seeking the advice of your support network, have a good look through the sheet music and listen to recordings to identify which aspects of the piece will need special focus.

7. **What are the most striking musical opportunities?** What grabs you about the piece? Try to keep your expressive goal in the forefront of your planning whenever learning music.

8. **Do I have a deadline?** If you need to be performance-ready by a specific date, work out the halfway point between then and now. Then, make sure you can play the piece accurately and with confidence by that time. This will ensure you have plenty of leeway in case you hit difficulty or need extra support, as well as time to "live with" the music and get to know it inside out. It can help to produce a simple plan **mapping out** what you need to get done and by when.

9. **What is my practice goal for today?** Once you have clear answers to all the above, you can devise your specific bite-sized goals for each practice session.

Start by Listening

When starting to practice a new piece, listen to one or more good recordings first if possible. Imagine it is you performing; visualize yourself playing the music and try to get inside the player's skin.

If it is a duet, ensemble, band, choir, or orchestral piece, listen out especially for the part you will be playing.

Make notes while you listen. Include ideas about the music, interpretation, performance, and any questions to later ask a teacher, colleague, practice buddy, music friend, or online forum.

You must **listen to music regularly**. Music, like any language, is first and foremost aurally transmitted. To be musical using only notation is a bit like trying to speak a language that you can read but have never actually heard. In music, we need to discover the expressive elements of tone production, phrasing, balance, rubato, rhythmic flow, voicing, and emphasis. None of these is fully revealed through music notation.

It is a huge benefit to hear new pieces demonstrated by a teacher, performer, or recording. And following sheet music while listening helps us to connect the sounds we hear with the music symbols written on the page.

Don't just rely on the recording. **Listen critically** with the notated music, considering elements such as the composer's intentions, meaning of the song, and performance traditions.

Knowing how a piece should sound also empowers us to accurately evaluate the quality of our own playing as we practice and progress.

Getting to Grips with the Notes

This section is for **beginners** and those just learning to read notation.

The teaching programme you are using should introduce notation steadily, starting with simple timing and just a few notes. A golden rule for developing confidence as a reader is to limit yourself to pieces that you can almost or at least partly play at sight.

Here are some tips to help.

- **Clap or tap the rhythms**. If you can perform the rhythm away from your instrument, you are more likely to play the notes in time.
- **Name the notes**. Try reading through the music without your instrument, simply saying the letter names of the notes.
- **Sing the melody**. Take this a step further by singing the pitches as well as naming the notes. Try to maintain a sense of the pulse (beat) and written rhythms.
- Throughout, **avoid writing letter names** or superfluous fingerings on the sheet music. This delays engaging with the notation.
- Try to **play the first section** at sight.
- Play the whole piece **slowly**.
- See if you can **count the beats** per measure (aloud or in your head) while playing.

Take your time, repeating these exercises three times (in any order) before moving to the next step in your practice.

Avoid using any stickers on your instrument (for example on the keys, frets, or fingerboard) unless specifically advised to do so by your teacher.

Chunking

Trying to sight read your way through the whole piece is unlikely to be the best option. Patient work on short sections is almost always more effective. But this requires some initial **analysis** of the music.

- What key is the piece in? Does it change and, if so, where?
- Can I play the scale of the key? How about the arpeggio or broken chord?
- Where is the loudest climax? How about the quietest whisper?
- What are the main articulations used?
- Do the time signature or tempo change at any point?
- Does the piece tell a story or have a narrative journey?
- Does it paint a scene or create a special mood?

Using these **holistic** observations, you can break down a piece into component sections or "chunks."

Now, pick a section (not necessarily the first) to start learning.

- Sometimes it helps to start with the **most difficult section** and conquer it. After that, the rest of the piece quickly falls into place.
- Other times, it helps to start with an easier section, thus building confidence.

Different sections of a piece may benefit from **different practice approaches** and will take varying amounts of practice to fully master. **Reflect** on the approaches you have used, what worked, and why.

Whichever approach you prefer, breaking a piece down will help you to practice effectively and make for easily **measurable progress**.

More About Chunking

We have just seen that it is usually necessary to break a piece down into **chunks** and then zoom in on **shorter passages**.

But there is still a danger of simply practicing each chunk of the music in order, without being productive in our practice. We can avoid this mistake by trying to mix things up and practicing chunks in different orders. For example:

- A different chunk each day, in isolation
- All the loud chunks, then the quiet ones
- Similar chunks grouped together to practice (e.g., where material repeats throughout a piece). Then, very different chunks practiced together in a group
- All the chunks worked through in reverse order
- Chunks practiced in order of difficulty (from hardest to easiest), before finally putting it all together

As we practice these shorter sections of a piece, we can also home in on the micro-passages in which we are discovering persistent problems.

When working on a piece, we will ultimately need to follow both of the following two processes.

1. Breaking it down: full piece ⟶ section (chunk) ⟶ passage
2. Building it up: passage ⟶ section ⟶ full piece

In each of these processes, it is vital to exercise a zero-tolerance policy towards even small mistakes or hesitations. It is astonishing how quickly these can become permanent and, consequently, very difficult to fix. As soon as a mistake is spotted, it needs to be swatted!

Once you have finished practicing a chunk or groups of chunks, always ask yourself what has developed and what you've learned.

Troubleshooting

When a passage of the music regularly includes mistakes, lacks fluency, or doesn't make musical sense, it is important to establish what is going wrong. And while it is right to be intolerant of mistakes, we must develop curiosity about their origin.

Where and why are we going wrong? Here are some questions you should ask that may help to troubleshoot the issue.

How is this passage meant to sound? Listen back to a recording if you can access one, spotting exactly where, how, and why it sounds different to what you are playing.

Have I correctly understood the notes and timing? You can check by reading the notation without your instrument; try naming or singing the pitches, clapping the rhythm, and double-checking for anything you may have missed on the page (e.g., an ongoing accidental).

How can I improve my technique to master this passage? Would the music work better if you used different fingering, position, bowing, tonguing, or took breaths in a different place? Is there an interval that is awkward to play with precise tuning or embouchure? Perhaps you need to take a step back and address the technical issue behind the problem in a scale, arpeggio, or study?

How does this passage differ from similar passages? Sections of a piece will often repeat with slight changes. It's important to be alert to what is different with each recurrence. Adapt and update playing techniques to match those changes.

Make select notes on the sheet music **using a pencil**, so that when you return to practicing this passage another day you can pick up where you have left off. Combine this with writing in a practice notebook or journal.

The strategies above encourage a curious, creative, and critical approach to troubleshooting. Above all, **avoid the mindless repetition of problem passages**.

Slow Practice

Many find that slow practice is the best way to commit a piece to both mind and body, thus enabling the development of bullet-proof accuracy.

Slow practice is not simply working on a piece slowly because we are unable to play it "up to speed." It concerns practicing the music **more slowly than we are already able to**.

Adjusting the tempo can be a safeguard against rehearsing the same mistakes each time we practice.

Considerations for Slow Practice

- **Posture and relaxation**. Is your body comfortable? How about your breathing?
- **Movement**. Sense the biofeedback from each nuance of movement when playing. Can you spot muscular tension building up?
- **Pitch**. Ensure that this is entirely accurate before building up to a faster speed.
- **Rhythm**. Make sure this is unchanged. (One way of practicing slowly is to keep the same tempo but double all note values, thus playing at half the usual speed.)
- **Quality of sound**. Is the tone beautiful? Are the dynamics appropriate?
- **Phrasing**. Does your playing reflect the musical shape and intention?

Contexts for Slow Practice

- When learning a new piece, chunk, or passage.
- When isolating short passages, troubleshooting mistakes, developing fine motor skills, or implementing specific techniques (for example an alternative fingering or bowing).
- When trying to fix rhythmically uneven passages.

- When practicing breath control, intonation, or intervallic jumps.
- When focusing on tone production and phrasing. Here, it can help to use exaggerated dynamics, as well as emphasizing alternative notes in the phrase.
- When trying to memorize a passage, chunk, or piece.

Some of these aspects of our playing will necessarily change as we speed a piece up. By practicing slowly, as well as building up to the correct tempo, we learn to be **flexible** in our performance and avoid becoming locked into a single way of playing the music.

Practicing slowly takes considerable **discipline**. We are all impatient to play the piece exactly as we have heard and may find ourselves magnetically pulling back up to the pulse that's already fixed in our imagination. This is where using a **metronome** can prove helpful.

The Metronome

Patented by the German inventor and showman Johann Nepomuk Maelzel in 1815, the metronome has been inflicting misery on musicians for more than two centuries. Used wisely, however, it can be a tremendous tool.

Wooden mechanical metronomes are still around for those who prefer the traditional aesthetic, although you can of course download a metronome app to your smartphone or tablet.

The metronome operates on the simple premise of providing a steady pulse at a speed selected by the user. (The speed is measured in beats-per-minute.) Digital metronomes are highly customizable and usually feature visual feedback in addition to an audible "click." Some even include an electronic tuner.

Wearable metronomes are also available. These deliver a sensory pulse as a haptic vibration on each beat.

The most important feature to look for in any metronome is a decent volume. The player needs to be able to hear it louder than their own instrument.

When to Use a Metronome

- If your inner sense of the **pulse** needs strengthening. Try clapping in time with the metronome before using your instrument or voice.
- For practicing the **rhythm** of a section. Again, try clapping first, then playing the passage. Select a slower tempo at first and build up the speed.
- When trying to develop more **even** playing.
- For comparing the **tempo** of one section in a piece with that of another (e.g., the sections in a sonata-form movement or the verse and chorus of a song).
- When progressively **building up** a tricky passage to performance tempo.

Using Backing Tracks

A growing number of method books and sheet-music publications now include backing tracks that you can play along to while practicing. These can include:

- Demonstration tracks
- Educational videos with learning tips
- Accompaniment tracks
- Band or orchestral backings
- Tracks upon which to improvise

Backing tracks often use playback software that will allow you to **adjust the tempo** to suit your practice speed and interpretation of the music. In some cases, they will also enable you to **change the key**.

Using backing tracks can have **many benefits**.

- The need to listen and stay in time with the backing track prepares the player for making music with others.
- The ability to practice with an accompaniment when alone enables single-line instrumentalists to hear how their part fits with others.
- Being able to hear harmonies underneath a solo line allows for fuller interpretations of phrasing and expression.
- Backing tracks can be more musically engaging than using a metronome and can help the player assimilate the feel of different musical styles.
- Using backing tracks can impart confidence when first learning to improvise and add enjoyment for those improvising at a more advanced level.

When using backing tracks, it is important to consider a number of aspects.

1. **Listen** to the backing track before you start learning the piece. This will help you shape your practice goals, understand the groove, and hear how your part will fit into the music as a whole.

2. If you are learning the piece using notation, **follow the written music** while listening. Try clapping the rhythm of your part along to the backing track. This will help you to develop your listening ability and learn the timing correctly.

3. Make sure that you have **learned to play your notes** confidently before trying to play along with the backing track.

4. **Use suitable equipment**, with a volume similar to that of live musicians, so that you can hear the backing clearly and play with personal confidence at an appropriate dynamic.

5. Even the most flexible backing tracks don't respond to timing in the way that **live musicians** will. Practicing with backing tracks **doesn't replace** the need to work with your accompanist or show up to band practice!

6. When playing with backing tracks, it is necessary to **conform to their timing**, groove, dynamics, and musical energy. It is important to use them reflectively and critically, recognizing that their interpretation might not be like yours.

7. It is important to **develop your own musical response**, which might involve considering aspects such as tempo and phrasing away from the backing track. This becomes even more crucial if you plan to play a piece with live musicians later.

Recordings

It has become easier than ever for any musician to record or film themselves playing. This can prove an invaluable aid for assessment during practice sessions.

Audio recording is incredibly useful, but **video** even more so. This is because it allows the musician to identify bad or distracting habits and reflect on posture, technique, presentation, and musical delivery. On the other hand, audio recording without video allows you to listen without the distraction of viewing yourself critically. There are clear benefits to both types of recording.

It can be uncomfortable listening back to recordings of our playing. But here are three reasons why we can benefit from regularly doing so.

1. Critical Listening

Our playing does not always sound quite how we **imagine** it.

Listening to a recording, we move beyond our self-perception and hear our playing from another **perspective**. We notice things (good and bad) that we otherwise miss. In doing this, we can also learn to develop a more critical ear.

We can use our recordings to **compare** our playing with other great players, reflecting on which aspects of their performance and interpretation we prefer or would like to develop.

2. Deeper Analysis

When we record ourselves, we can listen back with our full **attention**, not distracted by the business of playing our instrument. Different mental and aural processes are at work and our focus completely shifts.

A recording is the perfect tool for **analyzing** our own playing. We can focus on sections of the music where we have questions and concerns. We can follow the notation and look for discrepancies in our playing. We can reflect on whether our interpretation is working, both in the details and in the overall flow.

In a video, we may also be able to spot **physical causes of the problems** in our playing that we are working to resolve, just as an athlete will study footage to analyze strengths and weaknesses.

3. Tracking Progress

As we continue to record our playing, our **archive** of recordings serves as a useful reminder of how far we have progressed and how much repertoire we have absorbed.

General Recording Tips

- It is never too soon to start recording yourself playing. You could do so even before your very first lesson!
- Listen back to a recording several times, reflecting on different aspects of your playing (e.g., general accuracy, sense of pace, tone, and expression).
- Try to stay objective, as though listening to another musician.
- Try recording a whole practice session if time permits. Consider how well time spent, successful elements of your practice, and areas of improvements to your practice technique and routine.
- Consider sharing recordings for constructive feedback from a teacher, colleague, or practice buddy.

Practicing Together

A "practice buddy" is a person with whom you can share your practice journey, from comparing notes to encouraging and holding each other to account. Well, why not get together with your practice buddy for some shared music time?

Here are some activities you could include.

- **Share warm-up activities** such as stretching, playing long notes, tuning your instruments, and planning.
- **Share scale practice**. Play scales in unison, in contrary motion, or using different dynamics and articulations. Listen carefully to one another, offering feedback and setting challenges!
- **Listen to recordings** together, discussing and comparing your impressions of different music and performances. What do you like or dislike? What do you agree on and where do your opinions vary? Importantly, what can you learn from each other?
- **Listen to one another** playing a solo. Find two positives and one suggestion to encourage each other.
- Find suitable **duets** to play together. Listen to each other's part and then rehearse playing together. Use the principles of chunking, slow practice, and the other practice strategies discussed in this book.
- **Improvise** or **compose** a piece together.
- Make a **recording** together.
- **Organize a concert** for your families and friends.
- Overall, be **creative** and **positive** in helping each other.

How to Practice Mindfully

Breaks (A Guide)

Most will agree that when practicing for a stretch of time, it's important to take regular breaks. There is perhaps less consensus about how frequently and for how long. So, we must consider why breaks are necessary.

Why We Need Breaks

- Rest is essential for our physical health and mental well-being.
- We need to give our tissues and tendons rest to lower the risk of injury.
- Just as taking breaks increases productivity in the workplace, so they can increase the efficacy of our practice.

Research suggests that when taking a break our brain remains active, processing information, consolidating memories, and planning next steps. And in addition to all this activity, the mind needs time to wander, just as the body needs time to recuperate.

Taking breaks can improve your mood, boost your performance, and increase your ability to concentrate. If you don't give your mind a chance to pause and refresh, it isn't going to work efficiently and your practice will be wasted.

How Long?

Musicians should aim to have at least a 10-minute break per hour of practice. However, the absorbing nature of practice can distract us from this requirement. Scheduling 5–10 minutes to break from playing in each 30 minutes of practice is important.

Plan your breaks. If they don't occupy a specific place within your session, they can be easily brushed aside.

Sometimes, it may be necessary to take a break sooner than planned. The adage "no pain, no gain" is untrue when it comes to practicing music. If you experience any discomfort when playing, you need an immediate break.

If you routinely experience fatigue or soreness after playing, consult an expert teacher or performing arts medical practitioner for advice.

What to Do During Your Breaks

It is tempting to use breaks during a practice session to remain focused on music-making; evaluating practice, analyzing recordings, and listening to other performances for insight. But the mind needs a break to be refreshed, too.

To help our minds reboot, it can be useful to leave the practice environment, take a short walk around the block, have a snack, or make a drink.

Consider using a short break to do a few relaxation exercises and stretches. Done correctly, such activities refresh mind and body alike.

Breaks can be useful for physical exercise. This not only contributes to our well-being, physical fitness, and immunity, but also boosts brain health and can maximize the benefits of a practice session.

Taking time out for breathing exercises is perhaps the easiest way to boost both practice efficiency and personal well-being. Try the breathwork exercise provided earlier on page 30.

Silent Practice

Acquiring the ability to "hear" music in our heads and visualize ourselves playing a piece is fundamental to our success as musicians. It does, of course, take time to develop.

Silent practice can take on many forms, from playing "air guitar" to visualizing a performance. Here are some tips to help you practice music without your instrument.

- Read notation away from your instrument, "hearing" the music in your head.
- Sing the music you are practicing. It can be your solo line or other musical lines within a score.
- Imagine yourself playing the notes. Breathe and move as you would if you were holding or playing your instrument, miming and sensing the physical movements involved.
- When taking a shower, enjoying a walk, or lying in your bed, try to rehearse the piece in your head, hearing it as a mental recording. Can you remember the whole piece? How does the music impact upon your emotions?
- Study the score again, perhaps in a different edition if you can access one. See if you can notice details that you have previously missed.
- Take your music with you on train or bus journeys. Read through it, imagine the piece in your head, and even mime out words or fingering.

To grow as musicians, we need to saturate ourselves in music, both in sound and in silence.

The Progress Checklist

It is important to continually evaluate the effectiveness of our practice. Even a few minutes into a session, it's good to pause and consider if we are perceptibly getting somewhere (and, indeed, whether that matters or not).

For when you are ready for a slightly longer break, here's a checklist that can be used to reflect on your progress.

- Are you feeling positive? Having a good time?
- Have you warmed up effectively and what difference has it made?
- Have you played any active repertoire pieces? Did you enjoy them?
- What are the successes or problems in your technique today?
- Are you engaging with the music you are playing?
- Do you have any questions about the music you are practicing? Where might you find the answer(s)?
- When making mistakes, have you corrected them thoroughly? Do you know the cause of those mistakes?
- What have you practiced slowly today? And up to speed?
- Do you have an idea of how you want the music to sound?
- Have you made steps towards completing your goals for the session?
- What (if anything) is continuing to frustrate you, and why?
- Have you played anything from memory in this session?
- Have you improvised or created any new music today?
- Do you like the quality of your tone today?
- What tweaks to the next practice section are needed?

Feedback and Support

Whether you use online learning, attend group sessions, are self-teaching from a book, or enjoy the benefits of having a private teacher, there's no denying the importance of receiving expert support and guidance. Playing music is a shared journey.

The constructive feedback of a good teacher or more experienced player will help you to identify the best qualities of your playing and provide insight into how to fix any problems that are holding you back.

A trained ear and eye will notice minor errors that you will have missed, as well as being able to advise on the technical, musical, and performance aspects of your playing that require improvement. Those with a knowledge of the repertoire will be able to offer stylistic tips, too.

There are a number of things to consider when receiving and processing feedback.

1. Always thank people for their support, whether their comments have been positive or negative. Listen closely, don't interrupt, and be grateful that the person is giving their time.

2. Allow for the imperfection of the critic. However good the critic's intentions, sometimes criticism can seem more negative than intended. With that in mind, stay calm and don't react until you have had time to reflect upon what you have been told.

3. Check you have understood the feedback correctly, and request clarification and additional information where needed. Ask for feedback to be as specific as possible, referencing notation and encouraging clear guidance on how to improve.

4. Find encouragement in all feedback you receive, without being defensive.

   - If it seems overly critical, reframe it to be more positive and embrace the opportunity for self-improvement.
   - If over-positive, take time to give more weight to any hints, tips, or suggestions about how you can improve your music.

5. If necessary, schedule time to reflect on the feedback you receive. Use your next practice session to explore what you can learn from it.

6. Ask for a follow-up session or lesson, so that you can refer and chart your progress positively.

It is important to note that if you receive feedback that is consistently and predominantly negative, you should ignore it. Regardless of the reputation of a teacher or organization, it is unacceptable to offer a critique that fails to celebrate the positive strengths of a musician's playing alongside criticism.

Music is for everyone and that includes you.

When giving feedback to other musicians, bear all of the above in mind. Don't give feedback that is beyond your expertise. Be honest and humble about your own gifts and expertise, and always consider how it would feel to be on the receiving end of your comments.

Feedback, including constructive criticism, can be an enormous help on our practice journey. But for this potential to be realized, it must be both given and received with humility, grace, and musical enthusiasm.

How to Practice Playing

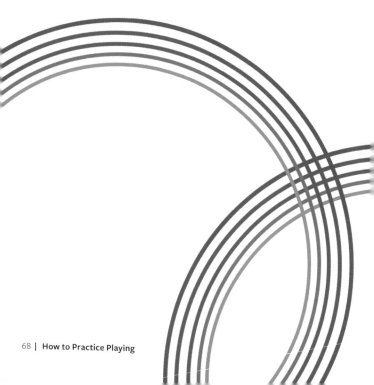

Playfulness

There are two types of practice session. Elements of the first, the "daily routine session," are thoroughly covered in earlier chapters. This section is about the second type; that longer "deep dive" into your musical journey, which can be more occasional, leisurely, varied, and absorbing. In this practice session, discover where your playful curiosity can take you.

Do you remember building sandcastles on the beach, searching for bugs in the garden, or trying to fly a kite? Play is the most powerful and transformative of all learning experiences. And if we can tap into that when practicing music, astonishing things can happen.

Dr Stuart Brown, author of the book *Play: How It Shapes the Brain, Opens the Imagination, and Invigorates the Soul*, identifies four key ingredients of transformative play, which we would do well to consider.

1. Play Justifies Itself

To be like play, practice must be done for its own sake, not to achieve a goal.

2. Play Is Voluntary

Play is neither a requirement nor an obligation. It is not timetabled or dependent on self-discipline. In fact, it is the exact opposite of that!

3. Play Is Outside of Time

When we are fully engaged in play, we can easily lose our sense of the passage of time. When we are absorbed by practicing, composing, or playing our favorite music, time flies by unnoticed.

4. Play Is Improvisational

This is perhaps the most important point of them all. Play is spontaneous. It is purely "in the moment" and doesn't lock into a rigid methodology.

Many of us find it difficult to transition towards a more playful approach to practice. We find it hard enough to carve out the space needed for our basic practice and the idea of spending a longer session playing purely for our own enjoyment can seem selfish. And then there's that list of scales, studies, and pieces, with looming deadlines.

It can help to make a list of all the things that we **think we should practice**, and then one by one cross them off. Screw up the paper and throw it away. Literally.

Once we've thrown that list away, let's play some of the **sounds we love** best on our instrument. Perhaps the high or the low notes, the quietest or loudest sounds. Just enjoy them, before deciding **with complete freedom** what to play next.

It is interesting and instructive to **quietly observe** where our play takes us and to later reflect on what we have noticed.

- Do we revisit the pieces we have loved playing in the past?
- Do we dig out new music that we fancy having a go at?
- Do we make up our own new music?

The answers to these questions can be used to **inform** where our musical journey takes us next, because it is when we play that we become the truest musicians that we can be.

While playful practice is at the heart of the "deep dive" practice session, we can start to approach all our practice with a more playful outlook.

Improvisation

Improvisation is perhaps the truest form of **play** in our practice, because it is simply about playing fresh musical ideas with freedom and intention. This has huge benefits for our overall development as musicians.

- When improvising, we often discover a higher level of **technical accomplishment**.
- Improvisation draws on and consolidates our understanding of **keys** and ability to play scales, arpeggios, and other musical patterns with authority.
- Improvising offers a context in which we can **express ourselves** without the restraint that comes from serving another musician's ideas.
- As we gain confidence improvising, we can turn our new skills of **communication** and personal **ownership** of music into a broader asset.
- The creativity we develop when improvising can be employed when **interpreting** other music, helping us do so with more authority.
- Improvising helps us to develop better **aural** acuity and to internalize music more effectively.
- When improvising, we have to **think ahead** and develop awareness of musical structure, harmonic outline, and expressive narrative. This deepens our instinctive understanding of all the music we play.
- Improvisation is **fun** and hugely **motivating**!

It's inspiring to use backing tracks to develop confidence when improvising. Excellent material is available for this, both in print and online.

Perhaps the purest form of improvisation is the **free improvising** that comes from a truly blank page. Try picking a group of three or four notes and a picturesque title or mood. Now, see if you can create a minute or so of music from this starting point.

Interpretation

With today's emphasis on perfect recordings, exam grades, and competition marks, it's too easy to forget that music is as subjective as it is objective.

- **Objective**, because some aspects can be assessed right or wrong.
- **Subjective**, because many aspects cannot be assessed as right or wrong. Here, reception depends upon the personal responses and connection of performers and listeners alike.

Where playing challenges our objective appreciation, our subjective enjoyment can also be undermined. But a failure to understand the dual importance of these complementary aspects of interpretation can leave us completely adrift in both our music-making and our appreciation.

Most tempo markings (e.g., "Allegro") are not exact speeds, any more than the impact of an accent on a note or degree of staccato can be mathematically defined. Much in music is left to the performer's **choice** and **taste**. This should be informed by the performer's wider knowledge of the repertoire being played (e.g., its historical context and performance traditions).

Music **conveys emotion**. As we continue to practice a piece, it's essential to be mindful of the possible meaning(s), the energy, and narrative we want to convey through our playing.

In most music, the pulse is likely to fluctuate a little for expressive reasons. The results we get when we are practicing with the metronome are not the endgame! We need to develop our own **interpretation** of the music.

At this point, it is helpful not only to consult the recorded performances of others but to record and evaluate our own playing.

Macro-elements of interpretation that we might consider when practicing, conveyed through our playing of the whole piece, include:

- Stylistic awareness
- Tempo, pace, and flow
- Sense of structure, narrative, lyrics, and climax
- Tone color and variation
- Global choices about dynamics and articulation
- General mood and energy

The player's goal must be to express the overall form, style, character(s), and shape of the piece.

Micro-elements of interpretation, conveyed through our playing of the details within each phrase, include:

- Articulation
- Dynamics
- Phrase shaping
- Ornaments
- Embellishments

When considering our interpretation of any piece we are practicing, it helps to have a good awareness of its **historical background**, **performing traditions**, and **our own reaction** to the music. We can then practice an interpretation that is both authentic and personal.

Continual, conscious consideration of these elements will ensure that the process of rigorous practice does not rob our music-making of emotive content.

Authenticity and Personality

Top performers approach interpretation from a variety of angles.

Consider the Composer's Intentions

Some performers are keen to get as close as possible to an exact rendering of the composer's original musical vision.

Such interpretation will require a very close study of the score, preferably in an **urtext** or variety of editions.

- For music composed since the dawn of recording, listening to any surviving recordings made by the composer or original performers is vital.
- To be historically informed, it is also necessary to research the performing practices at the time of a piece's composition and consider the differences between the musical instruments of that time and our own.

Accurately reproducing any composer's musical intentions in full is a challenge but offers a rewarding approach to practicing any music. Our playing will always require some compromise and should include an element of ourselves. However, it is important to develop our knowledge of how music has been composed and performed. This should be one key factor that informs our interpretation.

Listen to Great Musicians Play the Piece

Listening to music is the golden thread that runs throughout all effective practice strategies. When selecting and starting to practice a piece, you may already have discovered inspirational recordings of the music. Now, it's time to go back and have a more detailed listen, considering the finer interpretative elements in the performances of others.

When learning to play any music, we soon discover the problem areas, grow our own list of questions about how to play certain passages, and develop an interest in how others have met these challenges as players.

Feel free to assimilate or disregard the interpretative solutions of others.

Own Your Reinvention

We've first soaked up as much knowledge about the intentions of the composer/songwriter as we can. In addition, we've listened to the performances of others for clues about effective interpretation. Now, we can make informed choices about how to play a piece.

It is time to **own those choices** and to become as fully engaged as we can in expressing the music, bringing our interpretation to create a fresh performance that is **all ours**.

Developing Flow

A common pitfall in practice is that the learner habitually spends each session playing through pieces from start to finish. But there's an equal danger that those who are well-versed in practice strategy might actually never do this!

What Is Flow?

"Flow" refers to the extent to which a piece is performed coherently and engagingly from start to finish. To develop flow, a player must have control of the piece's individual components (technical, musical, interpretative, and emotional) and be confident of articulating them all within a continuous stream. For example, fluid playing will involve considering aspects such as tempo, pulse, rhythm, and momentum holistically and in relation to other elements (e.g., the piece's structural narrative). In other words, can you join the dots of your practice and perform with authority from beginning to end? Here are some tips on developing fluency in your playing.

- Perfect and try to **memorize** the sections or chunks of a piece.
- Check that all sections have a **consistent pulse** and that, where marked, you effectively communicate intentional changes in tempo.
- Practice playing the "**joins**" that link one section to the next. (Do you know where they are?)
- Play through your **mental recording** while reading through the notation. And then again, without any written music.
- Play the whole piece both with the **written music** and **by memory**. Notice any sections that go wrong and revert to practicing those chunks in isolation.
- Play the whole piece again, **repeating** these steps until you can play it all with consistent security and confidence.
- Begin to experiment with **different interpretations**, reflecting on how different sections take on a new light when they form part of the larger musical whole.

- **Imagine** you are performing the piece to an audience. Take a bow, introduce your piece to your imaginary audience, keep your poise as if on stage, and play the piece as a performance.
- Have another go at **recording** or **filming** yourself playing; reflect on the strengths and weaknesses in your performance.

Memorizing

The process of short-term memories consolidating into longer-term memory is known as **memorization**. This process is reinforced through repetition and by using a variety of learning strategies. Much of what we have already covered in this book will contribute to the memorization of music.

There are some specifics to also bear in mind if memorization is a goal.

Memorize the **smallest passages** in the music towards developing fluency. Then, connect these passages, recognizing **patterns** of repetition and change within the larger structure of a piece.

Be **consistent** in terms of **physical technique** (e.g., breathing in the same places, using the same bowing or fingering). Hone your movements to be identical with each pass of a phrase or passage.

Internalize the music. Sing the melody away from your instrument between practice sessions, "hearing" the piece in your imagination. In places where the flow and form are unclear to you, revisit sheet music to iron out those sections not yet committed to your aural memory. Listen to recordings regularly, with and without looking at the notation.

Playing a piece at a **variety of tempi** helps us to experience it afresh and will reveal where any kinks exist in our concept and memorization of the music.

Having memorized some sections of a piece, return to an **analysis** of the work's form and structure, noting how subsequent repetitions of any sections are different. Also consider how your interpretation will highlight the most interesting musical developments in the composition.

Successful memorization of music involves building up your **physical**, **aural**, and **visual** memory concurrently. If one fails during performance, another will kick in. Effective practice (using strategies highlighted in this book) will help to build up these different components of your memory.

Getting Ready to Perform

- Create a **timetable** leading up to the performance, with realistic goals for each of the preceding weeks and the days leading up to the event itself.
- When practicing, **visualize the audience** and all aspects of the performance (what you'll be wearing, what the venue looks like, how you'll respond to applause, etc.).
- Play through your music to as many **friends and family** members as possible, keeping to the actual programme and performing with poise.
- Try to include one or more practice sessions **in the venue**, so that you can find out how your playing sounds in that space and accurately visualize the performance.
- Remember, the **acoustic** will change once an audience is present, often becoming less resonant. You may need to **project** more than you imagine.
- Keep returning to **slower** practice, right up until the concert. This builds greater security and helps mitigate against encroaching anxiety.
- Continue referring to the **score** and **listening** to other performances, always remaining alert to fresh insight.
- Leading up to the performance, play a **mental recording** of the music in your head before going to bed each night.
- Repeat **positive affirmations** to yourself before you practice and imagine saying these to yourself when you are "backstage" and "onstage."

If we have been meticulous in our preparation, exploring the variety of practice strategies outlined in this book and by our teachers, we can have confidence that the performance will go well. Remember that our practice aims for perfection, while in performance we remain fully at peace that perfection is unattainable. If you are able to give just one listener a moment of transformation, even for a second, then you have done something very special.

Epilogue

I hope that you are now buzzing with fresh ideas that will improve your practice sessions. At the heart of this lies music itself; it is a wonderful gift that enriches our personal and shared lives, inviting us to become participants.

I also hope that this book will help you to bring all of your musical aspirations to life. In reaching towards these goals, your practice should not become simply work (a set of purposed, individuated tasks that must be done as frequently and well as possible). Remember, there is no shortage of evidence that the most effective way to learn is through play.

I am often asked how I can play by ear and improvise with confidence. Others ask me how we can teach these skills. Certainly, the theory and harmony knowledge, aural training, and practice strategies that I developed throughout my student years helped me to consolidate my learning. But fundamentally, the seeds of these skills were discovered and planted as a child. Most days, around 15–20 minutes into my practice, my mother would burst into the room shouting the immortal refrain, "Stop messing around and practice what your teacher set you!"

After decades in the music profession, I have no doubt that it was through my playful "messing around" that I learned my most enduring skills. Not only this, but it is through play that my intrinsic love of music grew and became the driving force of my life.

May you find the same joy in all of your music-making!

Andrew Eales, 2021